I Like Sports Stars!

Read About
Derek Jeter

David P. Torsiello

Enslow Elementary
an imprint of
Enslow Publishers, Inc.
40 Industrial Road
Box 398
Berkeley Heights, NJ 07922
USA
http://www.enslow.com

For Ed Heckel and all of my childhood friends who stayed true to the pinstripes.

Enslow Elementary, an imprint of Enslow Publishers, Inc.
Enslow Elementary ® is a registered trademark of Enslow Publishers, Inc.
Copyright © 2012 by Enslow Publishers, Inc.

Library of Congress Cataloging-in-Publication Data

Torsiello, David P.
  Read about Derek Jeter / David P. Torsiello.
    p. cm. — (I like sports stars!)
  Includes bibliographical references and index.
  Summary: "Derek Jeter plays shortstop for the New York Yankees. In his career he won many championships and awards for his outstanding play"—Provided by publisher.
  ISBN 978-0-7660-3829-5
  1. Jeter, Derek, 1974- —Juvenile literature. 2. Baseball players—United States—Biography—Juvenile literature. I. Title.
  GV865.J48T68 2011
  796.357092—dc22
  [B]
                                        2010029255
Paperback ISBN: 978-1-59845-301-0
Printed in the United States of America
062011 Lake Book Manufacturing, Inc., Melrose Park, IL
10 9 8 7 6 5 4 3 2 1

♺ Enslow Publishers, Inc., is committed to printing our books on recycled paper. The paper in every book contains 10% to 30% post-consumer waste (PCW). The cover board on the outside of each book contains 100% PCW. Our goal is to do our part to help young people and the environment too!

To Our Readers: We have done our best to make sure all Internet Addresses in this book were active and appropriate when we went to press. However, the author and the publisher have no control over and assume no liability for the material available on those Internet sites or on links to other Web sites. Any comments or suggestions can be sent by e-mail to comments@enslow.com or to the address on the back cover.

Every effort has been made to locate all copyright holders of material used in this book. If any errors or omissions have occurred, corrections will be made in future editions of this book.

Photo Credits: AP Images/David J. Phillip, pp. 22-23; AP Images/Elise Amendola, pp. 1, 18-19; AP Images/Bill Kostroun, p. 17; AP Images/Eric Draper, p. 6; AP Images/Frank Franklin II, pp. 4, 20; AP Images/Julie Jacobson, p. 22; AP Images/Kathy Willens, pp. 5, 14; AP Images/Kim Kmonicek, p. 21; AP Images/Mike Carlson, p. 15; AP Images/Nick Wass, pp. 12-13; AP Images/Tammy Lechner, pp. 10-11; AP Images/Winslow Townson, pp. 8-9.

Cover Photo: AP Images/Elise Amendola

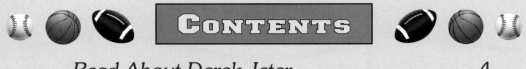

Contents

Words to Know

baseball—A game that involves hitting a ball with a bat and running around bases.

ground ball—A ball that bounces or rolls on the ground after it is hit.

home plate—The spot on the field where the batter hits and runners touch to score runs.

shortstop—The player who plays between second and third base.

World Series—A series where two teams play to be champions of baseball. The winner must win four games out of seven.

Derek Jeter was born on June 26, 1974. He plays baseball for the New York Yankees.

4

Derek is a shortstop. A shortstop needs to have a strong arm. He needs to throw out runners at first base.

Derek dives! He makes the catch!

The runner slides into him. But Derek still makes the throw!

This time Derek picks up a ground ball. He throws to first base. The runner is out!

Derek is great at running the bases. He slides into home plate before the catcher can tag him. Safe!

14

Derek also likes to hit. He is very good at hitting the ball.

First time up he gets a hit.

Second time up, another hit!

19

In 2009, Derek set a new
record for hits by a Yankee.
In 2011, he belted his
3,000th hit.

The Yankees won the World Series in 2009. Derek celebrated with his teammates. The team hopes to win another World Series soon!

Further Reading

Donovan, Sandra. *Derek Jeter*. Minneapolis: Lerner Publishing Group, 2004.

Tieck, Sarah. *Derek Jeter*. Edina, Minn.: ABDO Publishing Company, 2011.

Internet Address

Derek Jeter on mlb.com

http://mlb.mlb.com/team/player.jsp?player_id=116539

INDEX